WO

100 SOLOS
VIOLIN

Arranged by Robin De Smet.

787·1

WISE PUBLICATIONS
LONDON/NEW YORK/PARIS/SYDNEY/COPENHAGEN/MADRID

EXCLUSIVE DISTRIBUTORS:
MUSIC SALES LIMITED
8/9 FRITH STREET, LONDON W1V 5TZ, ENGLAND.
MUSIC SALES PTY LIMITED
120 ROTHSCHILD AVENUE, ROSEBERY, NSW 2018, AUSTRALIA.

BOOK DESIGN BY PEARCE MARCHBANK STUDIO
PRINTED IN THE UNITED KINGDOM BY
THE BATH PRESS, BATH

THIS BOOK © COPYRIGHT 1983, 1994 BY
WISE PUBLICATIONS
ORDER NO. AM33671
ISBN 0-7119-0355-7

YOUR GUARANTEE OF QUALITY
AS PUBLISHERS, WE STRIVE TO PRODUCE EVERY BOOK TO THE HIGHEST COMMERCIAL STANDARDS.
THE BOOK HAS BEEN CAREFULLY DESIGNED TO MINIMISE AWKWARD PAGE TURNS
AND TO MAKE PLAYING FROM IT A REAL PLEASURE.
THROUGHOUT, THE PRINTING AND BINDING HAVE BEEN PLANNED TO ENSURE A STURDY,
ATTRACTIVE PUBLICATION WHICH SHOULD GIVE YEARS OF ENJOYMENT.
IF YOUR COPY FAILS TO MEET OUR HIGH STANDARDS, PLEASE INFORM US AND WE WILL GLADLY REPLACE IT.

MUSIC SALES' COMPLETE CATALOGUE DESCRIBES THOUSANDS OF TITLES
AND IS AVAILABLE IN FULL COLOUR SECTIONS BY SUBJECT, DIRECT FROM MUSIC SALES LIMITED.
PLEASE STATE YOUR AREAS OF INTEREST AND SEND A CHEQUE/POSTAL ORDER FOR £1.50 FOR POSTAGE TO:
MUSIC SALES LIMITED, NEWMARKET ROAD, BURY ST. EDMUNDS, SUFFOLK IP33 3YB.

Für Elise.
Composed by Ludwig Van Beethoven.

Moderato grazioso

poco rit.

Morning Has Broken

Traditional

Chitty Chitty Bang Bang.

Words & Music by Richard M. Sherman & Robert B. Sherman.

Soldiers' March.

Schumann.

Pick A Pocket Or Two.

Words & Music by Lionel Bart.

The Ballad of Davy Crockett.

Words by Tom Blackburn. Music by George Bruns.

As Long As He Needs Me.
Words & Music by Lionel Bart.

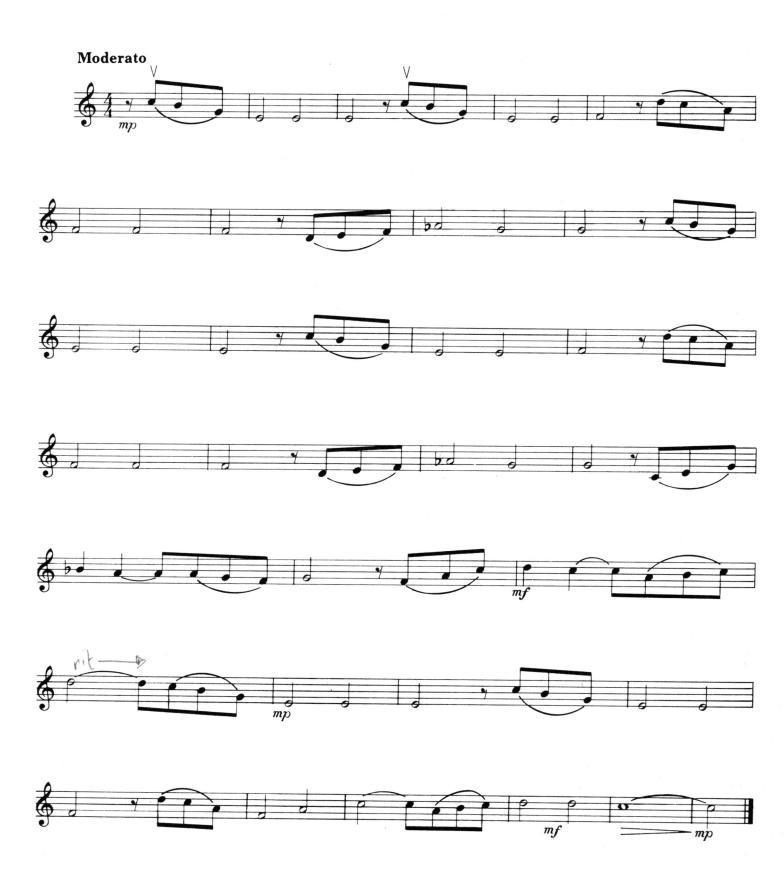

A Certain Smile.
Words by Paul Francis Webster. Music by Sammy Fain.

Where Have All The Flowers Gone.

Words & Music by Pete Seeger.

Moderato

Smile.

Words by John Turner & Geoffrey Parsons. Music by Charles Chaplin.

Andante

Love Me Tender.
Words & Music by Elvis Presley & Vera Matson.

Moderately slow

Scarborough Fair
Traditional

Moderately slow

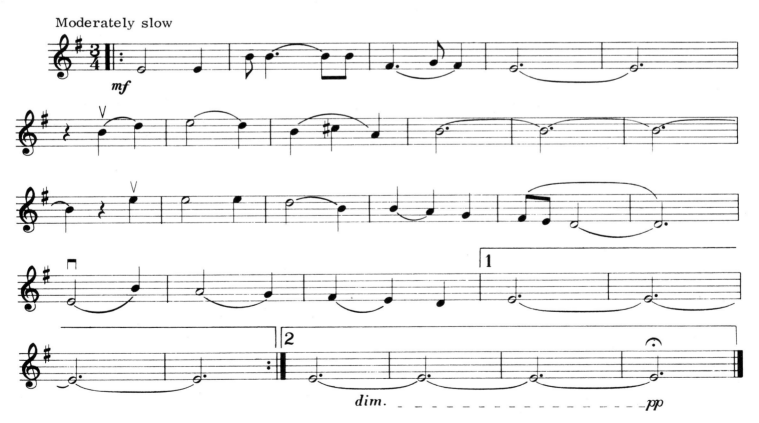

Truly Scrumptious.

Words & Music by Richard M.Sherman & Robert B.Sherman.

Broadly

Top Of The World.

Words by John Bettis. Music by Richard Carpenter.

Theme from A Summer Place.

Composed by Max Steiner.

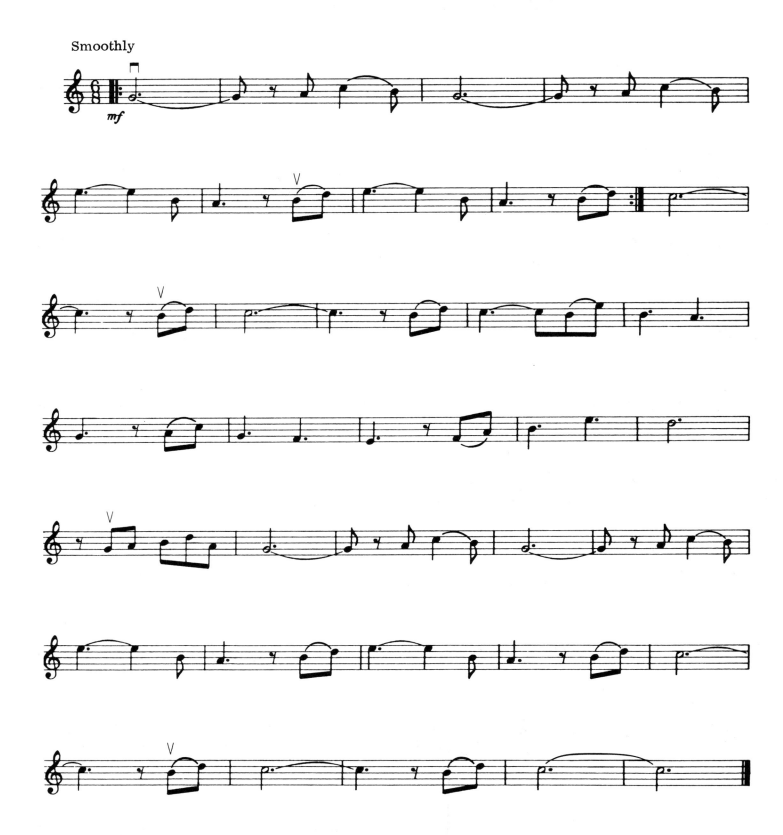

Sailing.
Words & Music by Gavin Sutherland.

Slow Beat

Minuet
Mozart

Minuet

Boccherini

Moderato

The Wonder Of You.
Words & Music by Baker Knight.

Slowly, with feeling

English Country Garden.
Words and Music by Robert M. Jordan.

Moderato

Oom Pah Pah.
Words & Music by Lionel Bart.

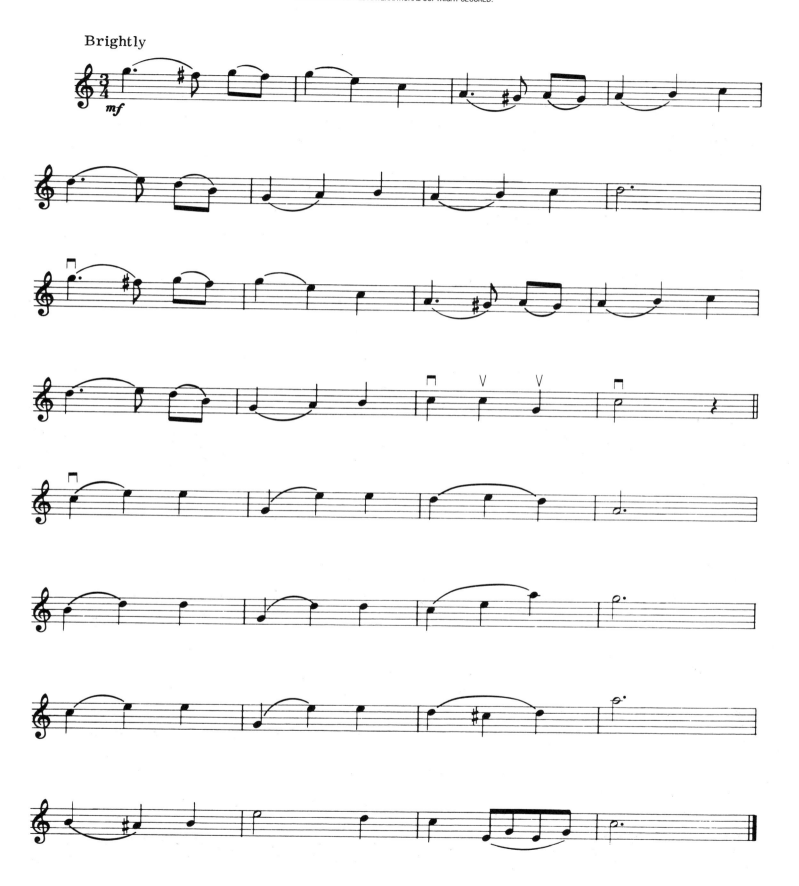

She's Leaving Home.

Words & Music by John Lennon & Paul McCartney.

Moderato

Mona Bone Jakon.

Words & Music by Cat Stevens.

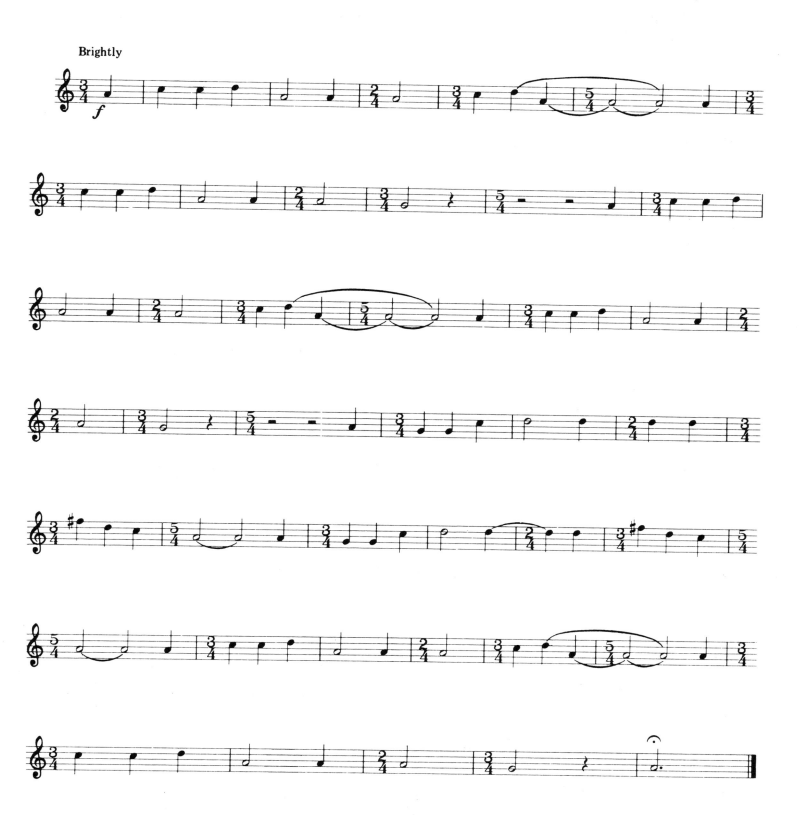

Puff (The Magic Dragon).

Words & Music by Peter Yarrow & Leonard Lipton.

Never On Sunday.
Words by Dilly Towns. Music by Manos Hadjidakis.

How Can I Tell You.
Words & Music by Cat Stevens.

Food Glorious Food.

Words & Music by Lionel Bart.

The Drunken Sailor
Traditional

Turkey In The Straw
Traditional

Bibbidi-Bobbidi-Boo.

Words by Jerry Livingston. Music by Mack David & Al Hoffman.

Light Schottische tempo

Michelle.
Words & Music by John Lennon & Paul McCartney.

Days Of Wine And Roses.

Words by Johnny Mercer. Music by Henry Mancini.

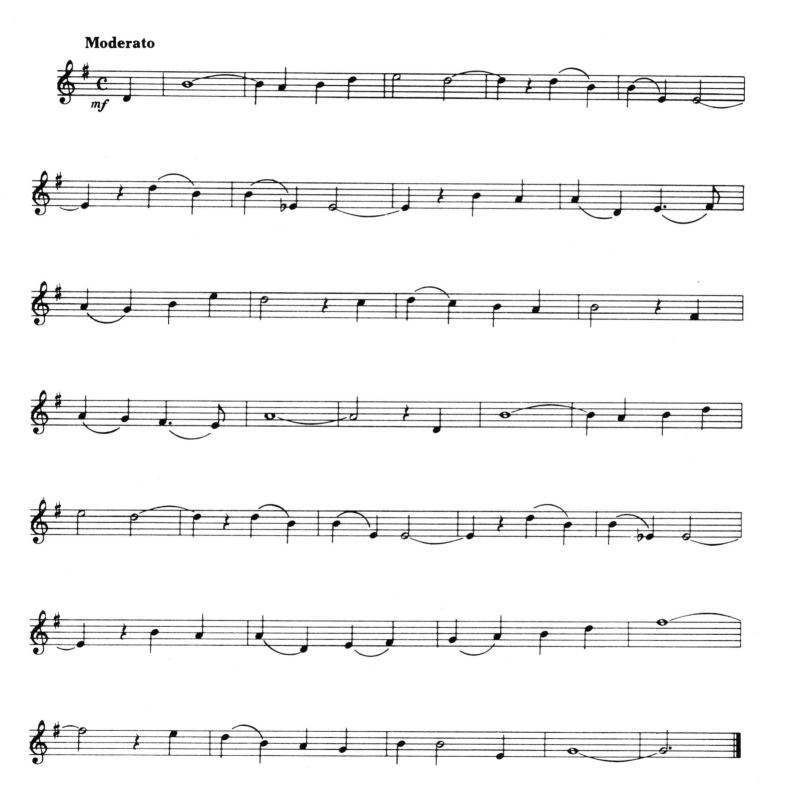

I'd Like To Teach The World To Sing.

Words & Music by Roger Cook, Roger Greenaway, Billy Backer & Billy Davis.

Going To The Zoo.
Words & Music by Tom Paxton.

Brightly

Steptoe And Son.
Music by Ron Grainer.

Moderato

Little Boxes.

Words & Music by Malvina Reynolds.

Moderate Waltz Tempo

In A Little Spanish Town.

Words by Sam Lewis & Joe Young. Music by Mabel Wayne.

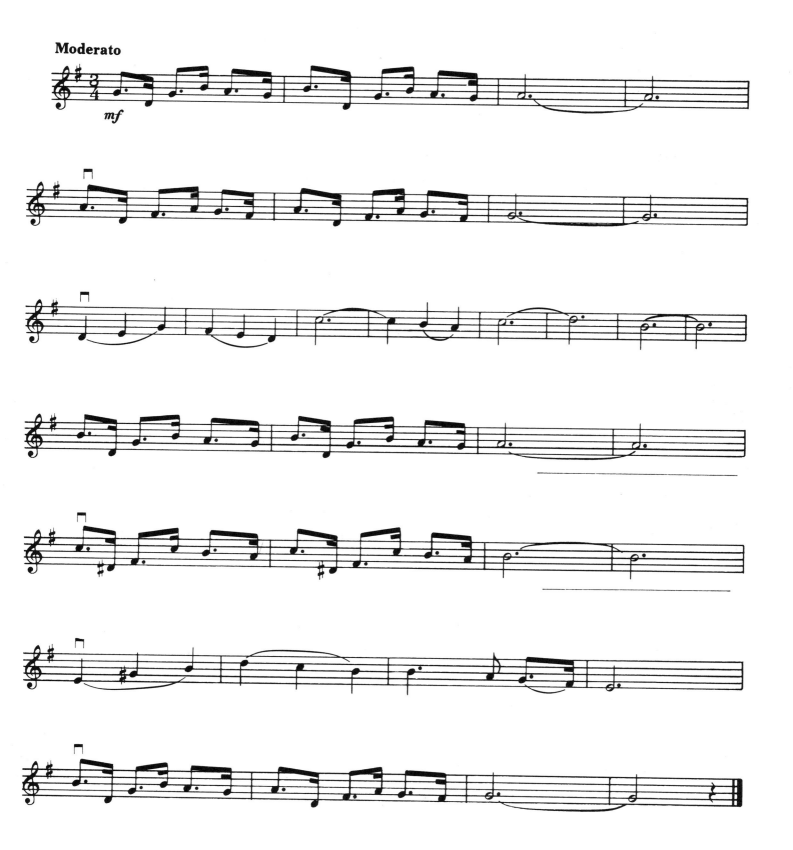

Where Is Love.

Words & Music by Lionel Bart.

Dancing Queen.

Words and Music by Benny Andersson, Stig Anderson & Bjorn Ulvaeus.

An Affair To Remember.

Words by Harold Adamson & Leo McCarey. Music by Harry Warren.

Moderato

Be Back Soon.
Words & Music by Lionel Bart.

Moderato

Be My Love.

Words by Sammy Cahn. Music by Nicholas Brodszky.

Why.
Words by Bob Marcucci. Music by Peter De Angelis.

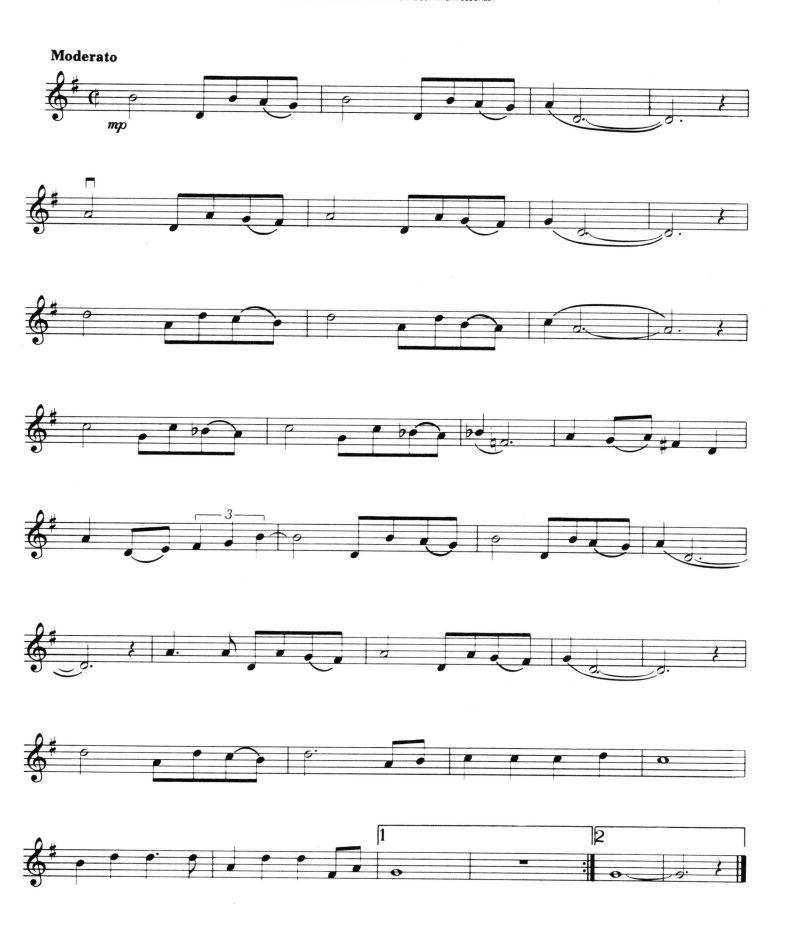

Strangers In The Night.

Words by Charles Singleton & Eddie Snyder. Music by Bert Kaempfert.

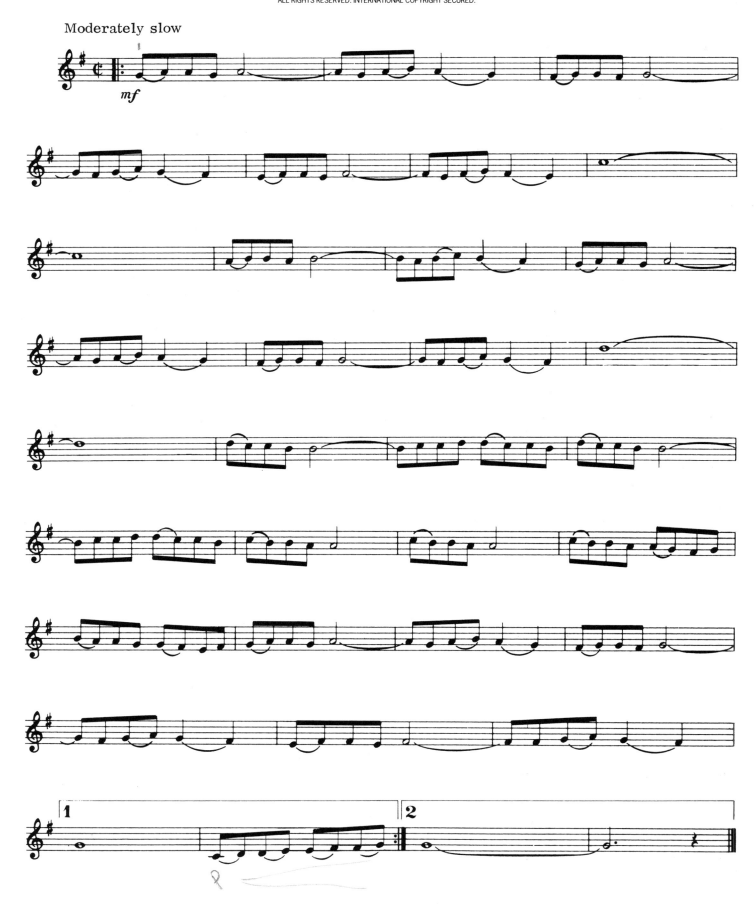

I Love You Because.

Words and Music by Leon Payne.

Waltz
Brahms

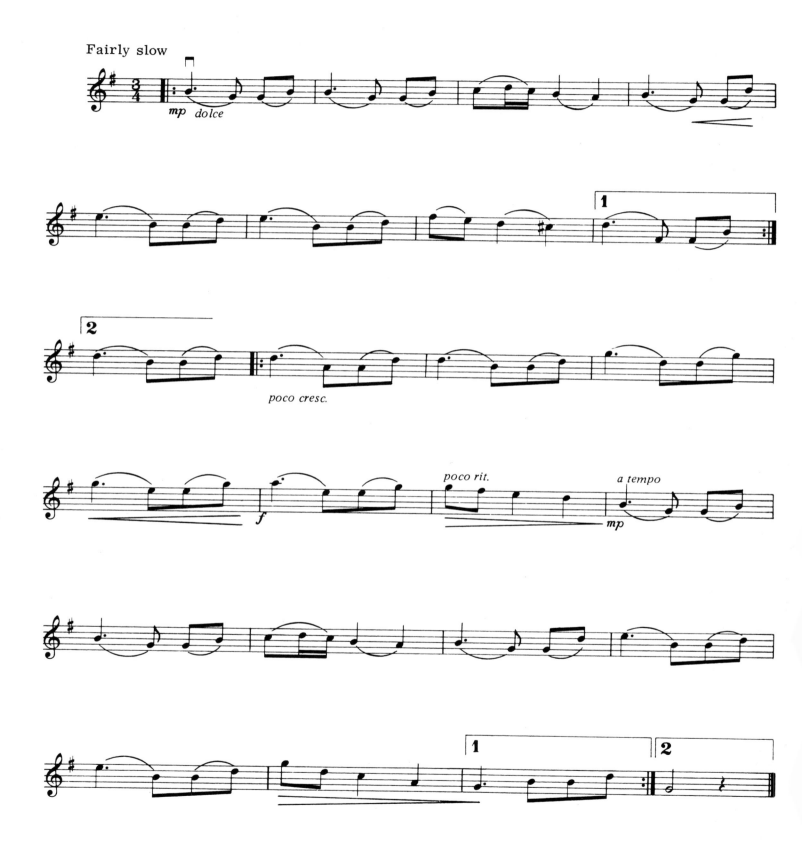

Norwegian Wood.
Words & Music by John Lennon & Paul McCartney.

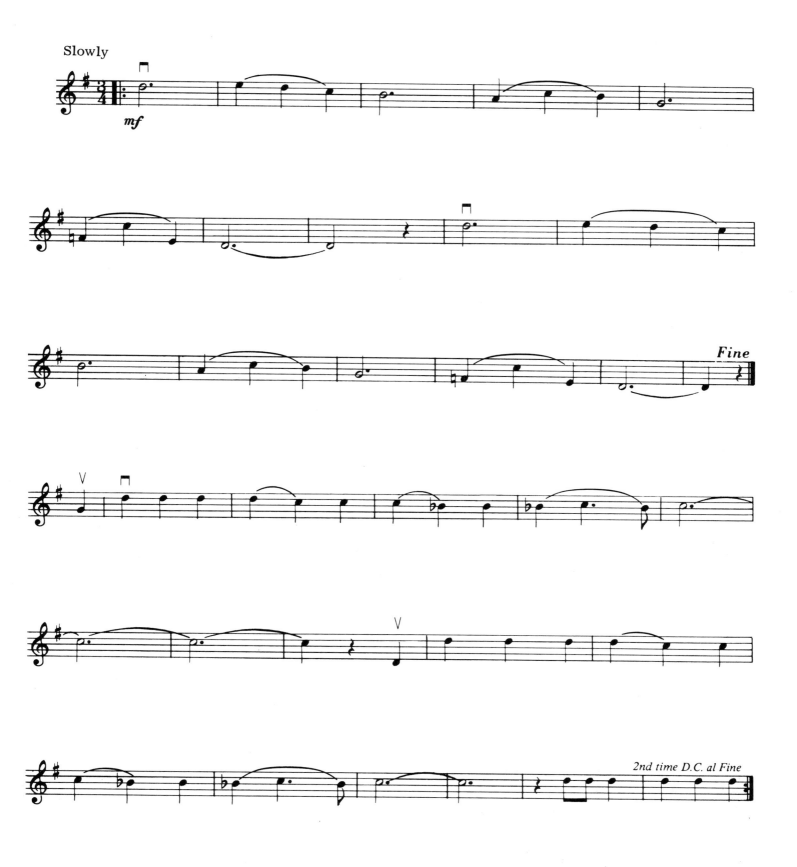

Somewhere My Love (Lara's Theme).

Words by Paul Francis Webster. Music by Maurice Jarre.

Mockin' Bird Hill.

Words & Music by Vaughn Horton.

Hawaii Five-O.
Composed by Mort Stevens.

Sgt. Pepper's Lonely Hearts Club Band.

Words & Music by John Lennon & Paul McCartney.

Let It Be Me (Je t'appartiens).

Original Words by Pierre Delanoe. English Lyrics by Mann Curtis.
Music by Gilbert Becaud.

Moderato

Wooden Heart.

Words & Music by Fred Wise, Ben Weisman, Kay Twomey
& Berthold Kaempfert.

Moderately (in 2)

He's Got The Whole World In His Hands

Traditional

Liverpool Lou.
Words & Music by Dominic Behan.

For All We Know.

Words by Robb Wilson & Arthur James. Music by Fred Karlin.

Moderato - with a light beat

Arrivederci Roma.

Music by Renato Rascel. Words by Garinei & Giovannini. English lyric by Carl Sigman.

See You Later Alligator.
Words & Music by Robert Guidry.

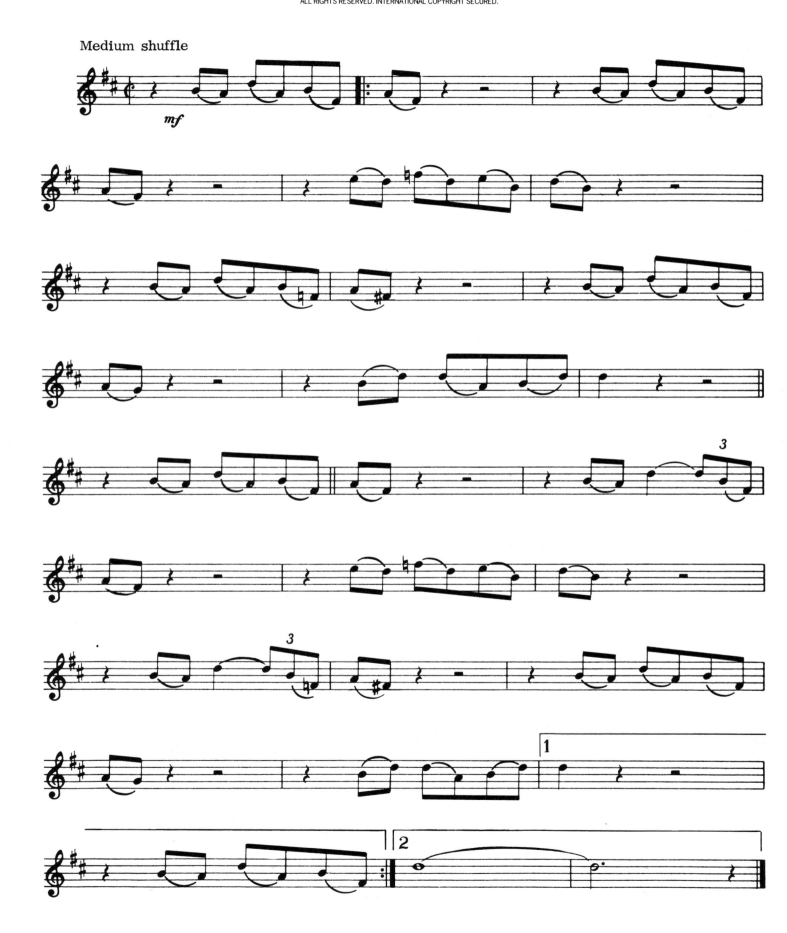

Sea Of Heartbreak.

Words & Music by Hal David & Paul Hampton.

A Man Without Love (Quando M'innamoro).
Music and Original Lyrics by R.Livraghi, M.Panzeri & D.Pace.
English Lyrics by Barry Mason.

Hey Jude.
Words & Music by John Lennon & Paul McCartney.

Rivers Of Babylon.

Words and Music by Farian, Reyam, Dowe and McMaughton.

Eleanor Rigby.

Words & Music by John Lennon & Paul McCartney.

Moderately

Danny Boy (Londonderry Air)

Traditional

I Don't Know How To Love Him.

Music by Andrew Lloyd Webber. Lyrics by Tim Rice.

The Fool On The Hill.
Words & Music by John Lennon & Paul McCartney.

Slowly

When I'm Sixty Four.
Words & Music by John Lennon & Paul McCartney.

Medium bounce

The Green Leaves Of Summer.

Words by Paul Francis Webster. Music by Dimitri Tiomkin.

Moderato

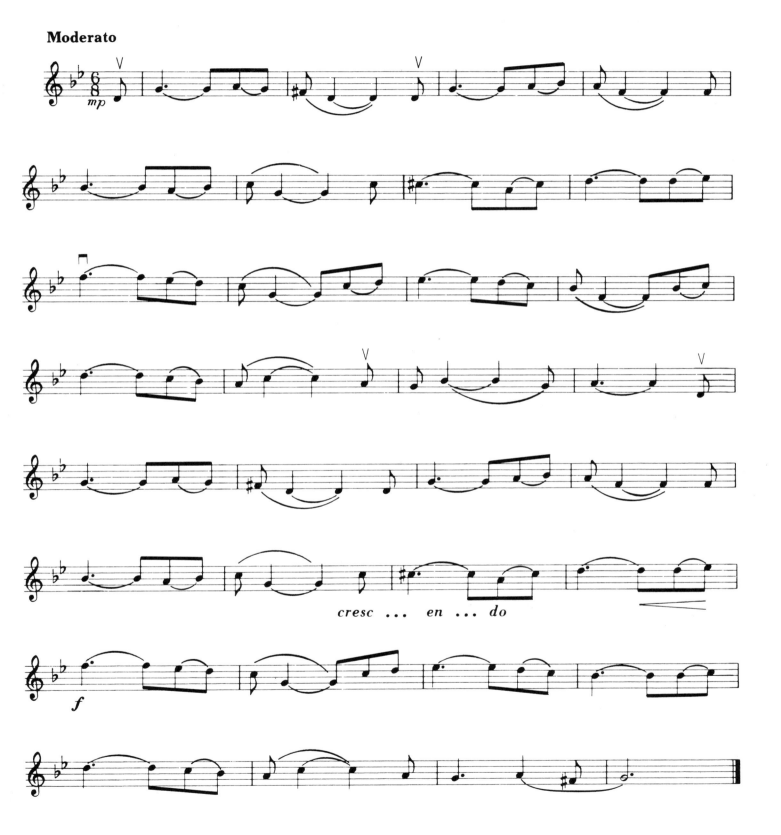

Sing.
Words & Music by Joe Raposo.

Lillywhite.

Words & Music by Cat Stevens.

Moderato

Return To Sender.

Words & Music by Otis Blackwell & Winfield Scott.

The Hawaiian Wedding Song.

Music & Original Hawaiian Lyric by Charles E. King. English Lyric
by Al Hoffman & Dick Manning.

Theme from Crossroads.

Composed by Tony Hatch.

Medium beat

Imagine.
Words & Music by John Lennon.

Moderato

Who Do You Think You Are Kidding Mr. Hitler?

Words by Jimmy Perry. Music by Jimmy Perry and Derek Taverner.

Consider Yourself.

Words & Music by Lionel Bart.

Fiddler On The Roof.
Music by Jerry Bock. Lyrics by Sheldon Harnick.

From Russia With Love.

Words & Music by Lionel Bart.

Moderato

With A Little Help From My Friends.

Words & Music by John Lennon & Paul McCartney.

Strawberry Fields Forever.

Words & Music by John Lennon & Paul McCartney.

Moderato

Reviewing The Situation.

Words & Music by Lionel Bart.

Moderato

She Loves You.
Words & Music by John Lennon & Paul McCartney.

Lady.
Words & Music by Lionel Richie.

Penny Lane.
Words & Music by John Lennon & Paul McCartney.

Who Will Buy.

Words & Music by Lionel Bart.

English Dance

J. C. Bach

The Entertainer.

By Scott Joplin.

You Never Done It Like That.

Words by Howard Greenfield. Music by Neil Sedaka.

Theme From Romeo And Juliet

Tchaikovsky

Knowing Me, Knowing You.

Words & Music by Benny Andersson, Stig Anderson & Bjorn Ulvaeus.

La Cucaracha

Traditional

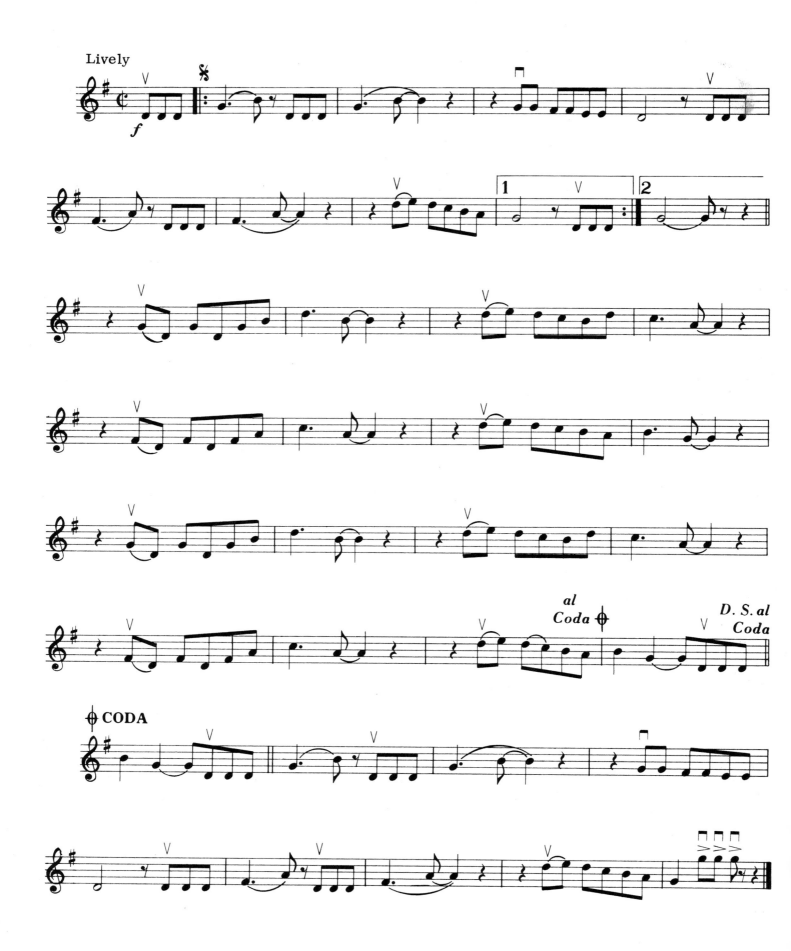

Thank You For The Music.

Words and Music by Benny Andersson & Bjorn Ulvaeus.

Hasta Mañana.

Words and Music by Benny Andersson, Stig Anderson & Bjorn Ulvaeus.

Jealousy.

Words by Winifred May. Music by Jacob Gade.

Singin' In The Rain.

Words by Arthur Freed. Music by Nacio Herb Brown.

Yesterday Once More.

Words & Music by Richard Carpenter & John Bettis.

Popcorn.

Music by Gershon Kingsley.

Moderato

All Those Years Ago.

Words & Music by George Harrison.

Mexican Hat Dance

Traditional

Lawrence Of Arabia.
By Maurice Jarre.

5/02(44185)